The Gospel of St. John as a Foundation of Spiritual Psychology

Robert Sardello

For information contact; www.robertsardello.com

Book and Cover design by Robert Sardello

First Edition: March, 2017

10 9 8 7 6 5 4 3 2 1

The Gospel of St. John

as a Foundation of Spiritual Psychology

Robert Sardello

Making a Clearing: Receiving the Gospel

Approaching the Gospel of St. John requires the sharpest of clarity. Our own yearning for the presence of its meaning isn't oriented towards theology, morality, or religion. And, if we wish to receive the gospel most fully, we must endeavor to hear it as if for the first time. Thus, any belief systems, or lack thereof, are not applicable in this approach to new life and the new hearing made available through this extraordinary text. Also, we won't analyze it, vivisect it or interpret it. Rather, our goal is to simply take it into our very being — an act concomitant with entering into the unique contour of *its* own markedly luminous being.

We're guided by the initial words of the Gospel: "In the beginning was the Word." What is this word, (Logos)?

Further, and most importantly, we seek to recognize that becoming aware of the Logos will simultaneously trigger an awareness of the Logos in ourselves.

The Gospel of St. John invites us to become initiated into an embodied, conscious soul life that is in complete communion with the spiritual world. **However, this experience requires a willingness to experience and perceive thought as a spiritual force. And, paradoxically, thinking is the only way in which we're able to consciously come into communion with the spiritual world — in the body, through the soul, and in the world. Not ordinary thinking, which is always 'thinking about', not the creative act, the Word, occurring and creating our very Being.**

The content of what follows is the product of the new kind of thinking. I am not here 'thinking about' the gospel, but from within it, a kind of awareness within thinking, thinking-awareness, which is attentiveness aware of itself. The content is the result of this kind of tending.

I do indeed recognize that this reading of John is probably scandalous, and I don't want folks who tread into it think that it is either spirituality or theology or anything of that sort – it is spiritual psychology. And, I more fully recognize that this gospel is indeed the true foundation of spiritual psychology -- as it is a complete concentration on the sanctity, really, of the ego. As such, it becomes vividly clear how spiritual psychology differs from all so-called 'spirituality' as it is more or less 'done' these days; and certainly different from the many, many, many, many disincarnating paths of spirituality. And differs also, completely from depth psychology.

Our working with the Gospel has precedents. The most important of these is the work of Rudolf Steiner in two important books: *The Gospel of St. John* and *The Gospel of St. John and its Relation to the Other Gospels*. Perhaps equally important is the work of Georg Kuhlewind's *Becoming Aware of the Logos* and Valentine Tomberg's *The New Testament and Covenant of the Heart*. The works of Kristina Kaine, while more derivative are wonderful attempts at phenomenology of the gospel. While we remain cognizant of their contributions, this is very much *my own work* with the Gospel that nonetheless recognizes the important contributions of these individuals.

Reading the Text

It's of great importance to spend time reading the text of the Gospel of St. John — several times. This reading is meant to allow us the experience of feeling the whole of the work, with its force and depth, and the way that it impresses itself upon our soul. The writing is far more than mere content; instead, it's sacred, even Eucharistic, in nature. Thus, the text must be approached on the plane on which it emerged. Put simply, to understand it, you must take it into the deepest recesses of your being. And, subsequently, you must allow it to transform you. How does the reality of the text live within us? And how do we cultivate it — and ourselves — so that it can live within us and we can live within it most fully?

The Reality of the Word

1 In the beginning was the Word, and the Word was with God, and the Word was God.

2 The same was in the beginning with God.

3 All things were made by him; and without him was not any thing made that was made.

4 In him was life; and the life was the light of men.

(In the beginning, which is always beginning is the Word, and the Word is with God and the Word is God.

All things are made by him; and without him, not is made that is made.

In him is life; and the life is the light of men.)

* * *

14 And the Word was made flesh, and dwelt among us, (and we beheld his glory, the glory as of the only begotten of the Father,) full of grace and truth.

(And the Word is made flesh, and dwells among us, (and we behold his glory, the glory as of the only begotten of the Father,) full of grace and truth.

How does the Word live in us? The Word concerns speech, but it also demands an understanding that the act of speaking, and is something that isn't wholly our own. It doesn't belong to us. Instead, it's a participation in the spiritual world that creates new dimensions of love in us. Firstly, a new and more vibrant "verticality" operates in and through us. We become a link between the earth and the divine and, simultaneously, we begin to operate differently on the "horizontal" plane as well. That is, we begin to understand our relationship with others in new and deep ways. This process, this rite of passage — even though it becomes deeply felt — can only happen by engaging within conscious awareness. This is a remarkable and unique contribution of spiritual psychology, the development of the capacity to engender a sense of speaking as consciousness that is simultaneously fully embodied and fully soulful.

What this means

People typically believe that their speech has no inherent connection to the realities about which they speak — and this misunderstanding leads to useless chatter. Thus, it's enormously helpful to become aware of speech as revelation. When you utter something, you usher it into the world. Also, this speech launches into every realm simultaneously and exists forever. Just as a physical vibration never fully dissipates, speech can never be un-uttered. Consequently, it's revelation that should always bear the imprint of the qualities of gift and grace. The act of speaking should be one with the spilling forth of truth. "And the Word became Flesh and dwelt among us as grace and truth." (*And the Word became Flesh and dwells among us as grace and truth.*)

Additionally, the act of speaking is always in the present. This is in contradistinction to the content of what we say, which always belongs to the past. We're forced to use words and concepts that are usually overly worn. And even if we speak of an event that is occurring "now," our speech can never coincide with the event itself. Thus, we always live in the past — in the content of our speaking, we remain perpetually removed from the present. Thus, if we focus on content, it's impossible to experience the living Word. Typically, we only experience the effects of the Word. Contrary to this, though, the Gospel of St. John initiates us into experiencing our own life within the Word, which is a perpetually vibrant present.

Thus, speaking oriented towards experiencing the Word asks that we become more aware of the "I am" in speaking. And the "I am" is present in our very capacity to speak. This means we don't have to say things with profound content — we simply have to be one with our speaking. (When you are one with your speaking, you'll discern that something more is present than your ordinary sense of self. You'll feel more than yourself, yet fully yourself.)

Exercise:

Bring your speaking fully into your body; speak from and out of a bodily sense of yourself; be present to the effort to speak as a unified being, to speak out of bodily presence, but also out of soul, from the level of soul. Notice that we ordinarily speak out of an ethereal part of ourselves. We operate from the "neck up," and we aren't fully connected with our words, or speech, or ourselves. Most speech occurs automatically. Still, the "I am" remains present in the act, but we aren't in communion with it. We remain distracted and enamored by content.

The Word goes beyond verbal utterances. It also includes gestures, as well as concepts, ideas contained within the Word, and is also the true reality of what is 'spoken about'. If, in this way of fullness we are approaching, I say to a person, "I love you", the words are the very act of the love. But because we aren't conscious of the generative possibility of concepts within words, our speaking becomes automatic, and we rely upon general and collective senses of the concepts within words — concepts of which we aren't even consciously present.

Stated differently, the Word doesn't have to be verbal at all. If I don't know Russian and go to Russia, in order to speak with someone there who doesn't understand English, we're able to communicate via gesture and expression. These, also, are Word. This is the case because the Word consists of the relation: "I-you-that." Word(s) are not things used to point to other things; they never serve as mere "pointers" to things in the world. The Word, instead, is a kind of syzygy of speaker, other, and thing. In the act of speaking, the relationship among these three beings is set in divine motion. The fixedness of the speaker, of the other, and of the thing, dissolves in the speaking, and what is subsequently present is pure spiritual act, but it's acting in an embodied way, in the world. The Word is present as the act of relating. **The word, the act of relating, is Christ's presence in the world.**

Note: *Presence to the word in the way described here takes place through intuition.* *Intuition, though, rather than a vague sense that something may be about to happen, is the fullness of the invisible happening within the visible happening.*

What has been said thus far may be difficult to grasp. We

can't know it in the way we know other things. At the same time, being able to dwell, to rest, in this intuition of the Word is the source of all healing. For example, when psychotherapy "works," it becomes effective when it steps into the relationship between the patient and the therapist, into the terrain in which the Word is intuited. Healing is sparked during a mutual, shared, experience in the spiritual world.

The Gospel of St. John can be read in ways that engender our capacity to dwell in that place of intuition, in the healing locus of the Word.

The Passion.

Please consider the following passage from a purely spiritual-psychological point of view. Relinquish all notions of religious or pre-conceived content.

13 Now before the feast of the Passover, when Jesus knew that his hour was come that he should depart out of this world unto the Father, having loved his own which were in the world, he loved them unto the end.

[2] And supper being ended, the devil having now put into the heart of Judas Iscariot, Simon's son, to betray him;

[3] Jesus knowing that the Father had given all things into his hands, and that he was come from God, and went to God;

[4] He riseth from supper, and laid aside his garments; and took a towel, and girded himself.

[5] After that he poureth water into a basin, and began to wash the disciples' feet, and to wipe them with the towel wherewith he was girded.

[6] Then cometh he to Simon Peter: and Peter saith unto him, Lord, dost thou wash my feet?

[7] Jesus answered and said unto him, What I do thou knowest not now; but thou shalt know hereafter.

[8] Peter saith unto him, Thou shalt never wash my feet. Jesus answered him, If I wash thee not, thou hast no part with me.

[9] Simon Peter saith unto him, Lord, not my feet only, but also my hands and my head.

[10] Jesus saith to him, He that is washed needeth not save to wash his feet, but is clean every whit: and ye are clean, but not all.

[11] For he knew who should betray him; therefore said he, Ye are not all clean.

[12] So after he had washed their feet, and had taken his garments, and was set down again, he said unto them, Know ye what I have done to you?

[13] Ye call me Master and Lord: and ye say well; for so I am.

[14] If I then, your Lord and Master, have washed your feet; ye also ought to wash one another's feet.

[15] For I have given you an example, that ye should do as I have done to you.

[16] Verily, verily, I say unto you, The servant is not greater than his lord; neither he that is sent greater than he that sent him.

[17] If ye know these things, happy are ye if ye do them.

The spiritual-psychological sense of the washing of the feet intimates an essential practice in coming to deeply experience the Word; it asks us to remember to care for the soul of others. As we walk through life, we acquire much psychic "dirt," just as in the time of Christ, walking on the dusty roads, their feet required much washing. And just as their feet required repeated cleansing, so do our souls. Feet are the most humble part of the body — and the soul is discovered most profoundly in the place of humility.

Caring for the soul of others

In order to care for the soul of others, we don't have to be psychotherapists. However, what we must do is pay attention to the soul level of our relationships. When we typically relate to another person, it's almost always on the ego level, or on the plane of ordinary consciousness. But relating to the soul requires being conscious, in relation with the other person, of what we can do, how we might serve the soul of the person — and this occurs **not after the interaction with the other person is over, but during the interaction, in the moment it's taking place.** Caring is a way of awareness rather than an awareness that we are asked or we wish to do something to care of another. The Word is the care; or can be.

Speaking-within-soul to another person requires an inner level of silence, of stillness, that fosters deep presence. This stillness allows us to be present in our relationships to what is taking place between us apart from the content that is being uttered. This doesn't mean analyzing or looking for something behind what is being conveyed.

Rather, it requires becoming aware of the pain, the hurt, the longing, and the self-closedness of the other — without being swept into it. Instead, we simply and truthfully acknowledge it without altering to suit our own needs or desires. Most importantly, caring for the soul of others is a silent gesture that indicates an acknowledgement that we owe our existence to the other person. Our listening in silence to the soul of the other is a filial gesture of instilling in that person, without saying anything verbally, that their being is allowing our being to flourish.

What does care of the soul of others do?

Caring for the soul of others constantly humbles us. And, in being humbled, we're inevitably moved into the profound recesses of the soul. Moreover, without this humbling, we tend to hover above our neighbor — often without knowing that we're doing so. The corollary of this is a lack of presence to the activity of the Word.

Thus, one highly significant insight given through the Gospel of St. John is that the act of attending to the soul of another being (not just another person – anything of the world, of nature, the animals, the plants, the birds, every creature, and Earth herself) brings our own soul to fruition. Thus, it's extremely important to know how to do this in ways that don't merely serve our own needs, especially when we're likely to remain unaware that this may be the hidden impetus for what we're doing.

Exercise:

When you are at the store, at work, or walking on the

street, when you have contact with someone — casually saying "hello" — while you are with the person, make an inner image of them and shift that image to the center of your heart and hold the image there for a couple of minutes. Then consciously erase the image.

Become aware of the quality of your heart-feeling when you do this with different people.

Write a careful description of the experience of holding three different people in your heart. What was the situation? What was the actual experience of "holding" like? What occurred in your heart? What was the result of this holding?

The Gospel of St. John: The Scourging

Then Pilate therefore took Jesus, and scourged him.

[2] And the soldiers platted a crown of thorns, and put it on his head, and they put on him a purple robe,

[3] And said, Hail, King of the Jews! and they smote him with their hands.

[4] Pilate therefore went forth again, and saith unto them, Behold, I bring him forth to you, that ye may know that I find no fault in him.

The practice of living within the image of the scourging is simultaneously a way of perpetually learning to remain free. And there are tree ways we lose freedom: One; By being pulled into some fantasy that removes us from the world: Two; By being seduced into an astute observation and manipulation of others (and of the world) with the purpose of bringing about something we think should happen; three; being trapped, unconsciously by some aspect of our past, such as lack of validation from a parent. These "prisons" are ways in which we avoid what the world brings to us, the very things we need to meet. To meet what the world gives us, to stand steadfast instead seeking ways around it, is our own experience of scourging. Again, to stand steadfast in and with what we are given is a strengthening of the connection of ordinary consciousness with the spiritual world. Remarkably, this also develops the capacity to be present in body, soul, and spirit to the Word. Additionally, it develops the capacity of conscious intuition. Such standing has to be with equanimity and neutrality.

It's extremely important to stand in and with what we're given and be present to it in a conscious way. This way of approaching "the given" isn't resignation, nor is it a self-centered kind of suffering in which we're aware of the difficulties of our life. Instead, it's a gradual realization of the type of fantasy that we usually dwell within and our urge to control things according to that fantasy. That being said, we never seek to eliminate these impulses; instead, we seek clarification by recognizing the character of these distractions.

Bearing "the given" is enormously difficult. And it's so daunting precisely because it requires a (very arduous) process of evolution. Imagine what it would be like to cease engaging in projecting, fanciful wishing, or figuring out ways to dominate every situation, or continually falling into our past — and to do so without any iteration of pathological resignation. Practice in bearing "the given" orients us towards being present to the activity that is the Word.

John 19:5-6; The Crowning of Thorns

[5] Then came Jesus forth, wearing the crown of thorns, and the purple robe. And Pilate saith unto them, Behold the man!

[6] When the chief priests therefore and officers saw him, they cried out, saying, Crucify him, crucify him. Pilate saith unto them, Take ye him, and crucify him: for I find no fault in him.

The spiritual-psychological sense of the Crowning of Thorns encourages us to reside in the realm of soul and spirit — not as an abstract belief, but as the actual practice of working further and further into a life that emanates from soul. And, if you attempt this, rest assured that you will be misunderstood. People will say you're being abstract, even though *they* are living in abstraction and you are living in the immediate present. They will say that what you're doing is foolish, and they will demand a practical definition of soul and of spirit. They will also deride you because your "soul and spirit" isn't connected with a large organization or religion. To bear this kind of misunderstanding without feeling attacked or "special" because of your unique alone-ness is the experience of the Crowning of Thorns.

If you persevere in remaining true to soul and spirit, then others will also be quick to point out all your deficiencies. While you will be working to bring something of soul and spirit into the world, to give something that can be of help to others, this is not easy and is not readily accepted. Instead, what is seen is all that you haven't done, or all that "should have been done."

This process of coming into connection with the Word has to be understood in the correct way. If the process is understood in any typical way, a kind of masochism comes into play. All of our fears, paranoia, delusions of grandeur, and narcissism can easily accrue to feelings of persecution. **However, Christ did not feel persecuted.** Feeling persecuted doesn't belong to the reality of Christ and it doesn't belong to the reality of the Word.

People simply don't understand the reality of soul and spirit because soul and spirit don't belong to **this world**. Or, more precisely, they do belong to **the world**, but not to the materialistic world, not to the world of gain and commerce, to the world of satisfying our own desires without considering others, to the world that sees itself fully and completely independent of spiritual realities. **The purpose of standing for soul and spirit is not to be understood but to be present, to be present to life. Nor is the purpose of standing for soul and spirit to convince others that these realities exist.**

("In him was life, and the life was the light of men. The light shines in the darkness, and the darkness did not comprehend it.")

It is also essential to realize that standing for soul and spirit will remain largely enigmatic, *even to ourselves*. It will perpetually be elusive and never fully understood.

Bearing the Cross

[17] And he bearing his cross went forth into a place called the place of a skull, which is called in the Hebrew Golgotha....

Reflecting upon the Bearing of the Cross can instill in us the capacity to love our own personality, the very personality that consistently doesn't understand soul and spirit; and it also helps us to refrain from entering into a hatred of the world that eschews the divine realm. For instance, we may constantly find ourselves not living in connection with soul, not being receptive to the spiritual world. We may find it too hard, too inconsistent with the world, and it certainly will never mesh with the needs of our personality. However, love of our personality doesn't mean looking upon it as a misguided ego perennially wandering about engaged in wrongful endeavors. If it were not for our personality, we wouldn't be in communion with the world at all. Loving our personality, thus, means working in the world in loving ways. Put simply, we're called to be the Word while still being fully in and with the world.

John 19: 17-31; The Crucifixion

[17] And he bearing his cross went forth into a place called the place of a skull, which is called in the Hebrew Golgotha:

[18] Where they crucified him, and two other with him, on either side one, and Jesus in the midst.

[19] And Pilate wrote a title, and put it on the cross. And the writing was JESUS OF NAZARETH THE KING OF THE JEWS.

[20] This title then read many of the Jews: for the place where Jesus was crucified was nigh to the city: and it was written in Hebrew, and Greek, and Latin.

²¹ Then said the chief priests of the Jews to Pilate, Write not, The King of the Jews; but that he said, I am King of the Jews.

²² Pilate answered, What I have written I have written.

²³ Then the soldiers, when they had crucified Jesus, took his garments, and made four parts, to every soldier a part; and also his coat: now the coat was without seam, woven from the top throughout.

²⁴ They said therefore among themselves, Let us not rend it, but cast lots for it, whose it shall be: that the scripture might be fulfilled, which saith, They parted my raiment among them, and for my vesture they did cast lots. These things therefore the soldiers did.

²⁵ Now there stood by the cross of Jesus his mother, and his mother's sister, Mary the wife of Cleophas, and Mary Magdalene.

²⁶ When Jesus therefore saw his mother, and the disciple standing by, whom he loved, he saith unto his mother, Woman, behold thy son!

²⁷ Then saith he to the disciple, Behold thy mother! And from that hour that disciple took her unto his own home.

²⁸ After this, Jesus knowing that all things were now accomplished, that the scripture might be fulfilled, saith, I thirst.

²⁹ Now there was set a vessel full of vinegar: and they filled a spunge with vinegar, and put it upon hyssop, and put it to his mouth.

³⁰ When Jesus therefore had received the vinegar, he said, It is finished: and he bowed his head, and gave up the ghost.

³¹ The Jews therefore, because it was the preparation, that the bodies should not remain upon the cross on the

sabbath day, (for that sabbath day was an high day,) besought Pilate that their legs might be broken, and that they might be taken away.

The Crucifixion calls to mind the ways in which drastic constraint opens up new capacities — if it is entered into freely and consciously, and without any sense of diminution. This is the reality-image of being held in place, and of waiting, listening, resisting an impulse to move. The crucifixion means refraining from attempting to convert others to our own point of view, even if it's the point of view of soul and spirit. It's the moment of surrender, of letting it be done unto us. Also, note that the cross is fixed in the ground; thus, it remains rooted in life. The mystery of the cross is something that works *through* our life; it's not something we must seek or find in the lives of others. Our task is to concentrate fully on what we do, rather than cause something to happen through what we do.

John 19: 31-42; The Burial

[31] The Jews therefore, because it was the preparation, that the bodies should not remain upon the cross on the sabbath day, (for that sabbath day was an high day,) besought Pilate that their legs might be broken, and that they might be taken away.

[32] Then came the soldiers, and brake the legs of the first, and of the other which was crucified with him.

[33] But when they came to Jesus, and saw that he was dead already, they brake not his legs:

[34] But one of the soldiers with a spear pierced his side, and forthwith came there out blood and water.

[35] And he that saw it bare record, and his record is true: and he knoweth that he saith true, that ye might believe.

[36] For these things were done, that the scripture should be fulfilled, A bone of him shall not be broken.

[37] And again another scripture saith, They shall look on him whom they pierced.

[38] And after this Joseph of Arimathaea, being a disciple of Jesus, but secretly for fear of the Jews, besought Pilate that he might take away the body of Jesus: and Pilate gave him leave. He came therefore, and took the body of Jesus.

[39] And there came also Nicodemus, which at the first came to Jesus by night, and brought a mixture of myrrh and aloes, about an hundred pound weight.

[40] Then took they the body of Jesus, and wound it in linen clothes with the spices, as the manner of the Jews is to bury.

[41] Now in the place where he was crucified there was a garden; and in the garden a new sepulchre, wherein was never man yet laid.

[42] There laid they Jesus therefore because of the Jews' preparation day; for the sepulchre was nigh at hand.

The significance of the burial calls us into a conscious understanding of entering into union with the Earth. This means that all we do with a conscious sense of soul and spirit is not for our sake, but for the sake of the Earth. The things that we do, then, with soul-spirit are done simply and without concern for any future results. They are, so to speak, buried. They aren't intended to be a success, or to make the world better, or different than it is. Look at this in light of your own work and engagement with the world and ponder the ramifications of what this means. All elaborate fantasies are abandoned and buried, but a larger perspective emerges. Naïve optimism is dropped, but our work remains unabated. In fact, a relationship with the world as Word is more vital than ever. It's likely that our task won't be appreciated or shared, but perhaps therein lies its distinct value and transcendent sheen.

John 20:1-30; The Resurrection

The first day of the week cometh Mary Magdalene early, when it was yet dark, unto the sepulchre, and seeth the stone taken away from the sepulchre.

2 Then she runneth, and cometh to Simon Peter, and to the other disciple, whom Jesus loved, and saith unto them, They have taken away the LORD out of the sepulchre, and we know not where they have laid him.

3 Peter therefore went forth, and that other disciple, and came to the sepulchre.

4 So they ran both together: and the other disciple did outrun Peter, and came first to the sepulchre.

5 And he stooping down, and looking in, saw the linen clothes lying; yet went he not in.

6 Then cometh Simon Peter following him, and went into the sepulchre, and seeth the linen clothes lie,

7 And the napkin, that was about his head, not lying with the linen clothes, but wrapped together in a place by itself.

[8] Then went in also that other disciple, which came first to the sepulchre, and he saw, and believed.

[9] For as yet they knew not the scripture, that he must rise again from the dead.

[10] Then the disciples went away again unto their own home.

[11] But Mary stood without at the sepulchre weeping: and as she wept, she stooped down, and looked into the sepulchre,

[12] And seeth two angels in white sitting, the one at the head, and the other at the feet, where the body of Jesus had lain.

[13] And they say unto her, Woman, why weepest thou? She saith unto them, Because they have taken away my LORD, and I know not where they have laid him.

[14] And when she had thus said, she turned herself back, and saw Jesus standing, and knew not that it was Jesus.

[15] Jesus saith unto her, Woman, why weepest thou? whom seekest thou? She, supposing him to be the gardener, saith unto him, Sir, if thou have borne him hence, tell me where thou hast laid him, and I will take him away.

[16] Jesus saith unto her, Mary. She turned herself, and saith unto him, Rabboni; which is to say, Master.

[17] Jesus saith unto her, Touch me not; for I am not yet ascended to my Father: but go to my brethren, and say unto them, I ascend unto my Father, and your Father; and to my God, and your God.

[18] Mary Magdalene came and told the disciples that she had seen the LORD, and that he had spoken these things unto her.

¹⁹ Then the same day at evening, being the first day of the week, when the doors were shut where the disciples were assembled for fear of the Jews, came Jesus and stood in the midst, and saith unto them, Peace be unto you.

²⁰ And when he had so said, he shewed unto them his hands and his side. Then were the disciples glad, when they saw the LORD.

²¹ Then said Jesus to them again, Peace be unto you: as my Father hath sent me, even so send I you.

²² And when he had said this, he breathed on them, and saith unto them, Receive ye the Holy Ghost:

²³ Whose soever sins ye remit, they are remitted unto them; and whose soever sins ye retain, they are retained.

²⁴ But Thomas, one of the twelve, called Didymus, was not with them when Jesus came.

²⁵ The other disciples therefore said unto him, We have seen the LORD. But he said unto them, Except I shall see in his hands the print of the nails, and put my finger into the print of the nails, and thrust my hand into his side, I will not believe.

²⁶ And after eight days again his disciples were within, and Thomas with them: then came Jesus, the doors being shut, and stood in the midst, and said, Peace be unto you.

²⁷ Then saith he to Thomas, Reach hither thy finger, and behold my hands; and reach hither thy hand, and thrust it into my side: and be not faithless, but believing.

²⁸ And Thomas answered and said unto him, My LORD and my God.

²⁹ Jesus saith unto him, Thomas, because thou hast seen me, thou hast believed: blessed are they that have not seen, and yet have believed.

[30] And many other signs truly did Jesus in the presence of his disciples, which are not written in this book:

From our perspective, a reading of the resurrection doesn't mean that everything turns out well. This is opposed to the usual adage, "Easter Sunday always follows Good Friday." Even if we enter into the inner development toward the Word, it's likely that our path won't be a smooth one. In fact, that kind of expectation is actually merely a new guise for egotism that narrows and guides the broader episodic narrative. Moreover, our ordinary consciousness can't discern the meaning of the Resurrection of Christ. However, if we experience it through interior imaging, it becomes increasingly accessible.

This is central: the resurrection concerns a new consciousness, not a new content of consciousness. Thus, it's fitting that the resurrection took place on the first day of the week. This intimates a symbolic newness, perhaps even a new beginning for a new humanity. And it's Mary Magdalene that recognizes the risen Christ, yet she does so only when Christ speaks to her. Before that, she sees Christ but thinks he's a gardener. When Christ speaks to Mary Magdalene, he makes it possible for her to see. This is truly a union — a union of spirit and soul; a new soul-spirit consciousness; and a new embodied soul-spirit consciousness.

Write a description of an event in your life that exemplifies each of the following processes understood as soul images.

1.The Scourging

2. The Crowning of Thorns

3. Bearing the Cross

4.The Crucifixion

5.The Burial

6.The Resurrection

Re-Visioning Ego

From Rudolf Steiner, *The Gospel of St. John and its Relation to the other Gospels:*

"Looking at the various things around us — things we see with our eyes, touch with our hands — we observe them coming into being and perishing. We see the flower, the whole annual plant life, come up and then wither; and though there are such things in the world as rocks and mountains that seem to defy the centuries we need only consider the proverb, "a steady drip hollows out the rock" to realize that the human soul senses the laws of transience as governing even the majestic boulders and mountains. And we know that even what is built of the elements comes into being and perishes: not only what we call our corporeality, but what we know as our perishable ego is engendered and then passes. But those who know how a spiritual world can be reached know also that this is not attained by means of eyes or ears or other senses, but by the path of awakening, of rebirth, of initiation.

And what is it that is reborn? When a man observes his inner self he finally comes to realize that what he sees there is that to which he says "I". Its very name differentiates it from anything in the outer world. To everything in the outer world a name can be applied externally. Everyone can call a table a table or a clock a clock; but never in the world could the name "I" fall on our ear if it were intended to denote ourself, for "I" must be spoken within us: to everyone else we are a "you". This in itself shows us that our ego-being is distinct from all else that is in or around us.... (and) within this ego another, a higher ego is born, as the child is born of the mother."

This passage indicates something of great importance. Finding a way to consciously participate with the Word has to be done without bypassing ego consciousness. In all other approaches to the development of spiritual consciousness, the ego is always circumvented. It's avoided, put to sleep, hypnotized, lost in a group, jettisoned in a ritual, weakened, and declared to be the source of all our problems. However, awakening to the Word concerns immediately recognizing the distinctness of our "I" — and then realizing that this "I" is mother to the "I" that is the Christ within us, the Word, the Life, the Light.

Thus, the seven ways in which we worked with the passion of Christ can't be understood as various means of ridding ourselves of ego consciousness. Rather, the passion of Christ can be understood as an enhancement of the ego, an impregnating of the ego. It can bring our ego into conjunction with both the deeper levels of soul life and the higher levels of spiritual experience. That being said, it takes seven miracles to keep the ego aligned with soul and spirit. Thus, the seven miracles in the Gospel of St. John give us a means of developing the capacity to be present to the divine with regard to the act of speech.

Interiorizing the ego

Our ordinary ego consciousness, it can be said, has no interior. Ego consciousness can be imagined as a flat plane. If we pay attention to the way in which we ordinarily speak, using the word "I," it is immediately understood that this "I" functions without interiority. For example, "I want to go to the store." Here the "I" speaks for some need (perhaps a desire for bread, or a desire to be with other people, or some unknown desire). "I love God." Here the "I" speaks for a spiritual level of experience. "I think we should consider all our options before making a decision." Here the "I" speaks for a level of personal opinion. In all of these instances, the "I" needs something outside of itself in order to affirm itself to itself. There is nothing within the ego, no interior light, no interior knowing, through which the ego can know itself. The ordinary sense of the ego must decrease. ("He must increase, but I must decrease." (John 3:30) This ordinary ego consciousness knows nothing in itself; it relies upon the illusion of an "outside" for its existence, and this illusion includes a notion that this "outside" exists apart from our own being.

Another quality of ego consciousness is that it is always oriented towards its own self-interest. This quality is not to be deprecated; it expresses the basic reality of ego and its association with individuality. "My interests are not those of the other individual." However, this individuality is but an imitation of a different sort of individuality, a spiritual individuality.

Concomitant with ordinary ego consciousness, there is the enclosed soul, the soul that leads its own autonomous life, made up of "complexes" and archetypes. Thus, the "I" and the soul occupy our lives in quite disparate ways. For instance, the soul provides an ongoing sense of interiority, even though we have little ingress into it except in the form of dreams, fantasies, imaginations, feelings, and pathologies.

The soul, though, is rootless. It lacks the certainty of the "I." And, lacking in certainty, explosions of soul occur in the form of fear, hatred, and cruelty. Also, the "I" of ordinary consciousness also lacks complete certainty. It relies upon what is outside of it to give it a sense of existence and feeling.

The healing of this split is attempted by Jungian psychology, but it's often taken in a misguided direction. For instance, there's often an attempt to "integrate" the "contents" of the unconscious by making it available to ordinary "I" consciousness. But ordinary ego consciousness can only know this content as something separate from itself; thus, integration means "knowing about" the soul from the viewpoint of ego consciousness. Archetypal psychology takes the opposite approach; it seeks to initiate ego into soul consciousness.

There are other spheres of thought that need additional clarification. In many spiritual traditions, and in current 'New Age' writings, there is a lower ego and a higher ego. This is the kind of thinking to which we've become accustomed and we're also generally persuaded that we should aspire to exit our lower ego and aspire towards our higher ego. It leads one to believe that we're able to bounce back and forth between two spheres, between the lower and higher egos. The statement from Steiner quoted above also carries a sense of two egos, but only if it's not closely read. He says, in effect, that out of the lower ego a higher ego is born. His verbiage is actually quite insightful; it encourages a vast and deep appreciation for the ego, and it helps us realize that there is extraordinary "ego work" to be accomplished!

The description of ego given thus far, it has to be said, is far too static. It operates as a kind of atomistic view of the ego, as if it were a static point, needing what is not ego to affirm its own existence. We have to take this image and confer upon it greater nuance. The ego isn't a thing, nor is it an idea. Ego is a no-thing. It is a no-thing that creates itself in relationship with everything else that gives it a sense of being some-thing. *Ego is a mortal creator.*

The way the ego gives birth to the experience of the immortal ego described by the Gospel of St. John involves putting the ordinary ego through some rigorous practices — the first, being the seven-fold practices described by the passion of Christ. These practices intensify the ego, which doesn't mean that we become more egotistical. Rather, through them, ego consciousness comes into its own and ceases to thrive on every-thing that is not ego.

Closely associated with the practices described as the passion of Christ are a series of "helps" that we've been given. These "helps" are described in the Gospel of St. John as the seven miracles of Christ. These miracles now live within us. Let us look, then, at their spiritual-psychological significance. How do these miracles live in us? What do they do? How are we able to come into connection with the modes of consciousness of each of the miracles? And how do they work in an inner way to bring about a transformation of ego into spiritual ego?

The seven miracles, understood deeply, are a vital means of healing the ego. They heal the ego because they heal the world through the innermost core of the world itself, the human being. Put differently, the seven miracles heal the ego because they describe the necessary process of deepening the interiorizing of the ego. Even further, the interiorizing of the ego is the nothing less than the revelation of the ego as an act of love.

The Seven Miracles in the Gospel of St. John: Seven Ways of Re-visioning Ego

The Marriage Feast at Cana (John 2.1-11) — (I am the Vine)

And the third day there was a marriage in Cana of Galilee; and the mother of Jesus was there:

2 And both Jesus was called, and his disciples, to the marriage.

3 And when they wanted wine, the mother of Jesus saith unto him, They have no wine.

4 Jesus saith unto her, Woman, what have I to do with thee? mine hour is not yet come.

5 His mother saith unto the servants, Whatsoever he saith unto you, do it.

6 And there were set there six waterpots of stone, after the manner of the purifying of the Jews, containing two or three firkins apiece.

⁷ Jesus saith unto them, Fill the waterpots with water. And they filled them up to the brim.

⁸ And he saith unto them, Draw out now, and bear unto the governor of the feast. And they bare it.

⁹ When the ruler of the feast had tasted the water that was made wine, and knew not whence it was: (but the servants which drew the water knew;) the governor of the feast called the bridegroom,

¹⁰ And saith unto him, Every man at the beginning doth set forth good wine; and when men have well drunk, then that which is worse: but thou hast kept the good wine until now.

¹¹ This beginning of miracles did Jesus in Cana of Galilee, and manifested forth his glory; and his disciples believed on him.

We are told in the Gospel, "There was a marriage in Cana of Galilee." A marriage, of course, brings people together, and when Rudolf Steiner addresses this occasion, he places particular importance on the meaning of "Galilee." He states, "It was in Galilee that the ancient blood ties were severed, that mutually alien bloods came together.... Christ's task was intimately connected with this mixing of blood. So, we are here dealing with a union having the object of creating progeny among people who are no longer related by blood."

The setting of this miracle can be understood as a healing of ego, as a further interiorizing of ego; it concerns ego engaged in intimacy with others that is based upon motives apart from self-interest. In other words, a genuine concern for another person is exhibited, and this is precisely the kind of love that is necessary to advance the process of interiorizing the ego.

Exercise:

Meditate upon the change from water to wine. Viewed in terms of soul life, it is a change from a soul element (water) to a spiritual-soul element (wine). This change comes about in the Gospel through the request of Mary, or, more precisely, through the relationship of Christ *with* Mary. Moreover, Mary's role in spiritual-psychological sense indicates that soul is the mother of the spiritual "I." Her motherly love serves as a bridge between egotistical love — love with one's own self-interests being central — to a new kind of love that flares with the capacity to love someone selflessly.

We might consider the following: Mary, with her suffering and grief, is the deepest embodiment of soul and she gives birth to the highest possibilities of the ego. Recall the image of Mary, standing at the foot of the cross. In other words, grief stands at the deepest level of soul — and that is where the image of Christ resides. Thus, if we move into the deepest level of the soul, a healing of the ego will occur, and we will enjoy the capacity of relating to others without seeking fulfillment of our own needs. *This* is a miracle. It's a miracle because it's something that transcends the capacity of ego consciousness. However, this miracle of Christ, in conjunction with Mary, lives within Soul as an archetypal soul reality. It's of great interest to note that Steiner indicates that this miracle can only be enacted *with* Mary. Something passes from Mary to Christ that makes it possible for Him to transform water into wine. Understood from the soul point of view, this means that spirit can't work in the world except through the deepest presence of soul.

The Healing of the Nobleman's Son (John 4.46-54) — (I am the Way, the Truth, and the Life)

⁴⁶ So Jesus came again into Cana of Galilee, where he made the water wine. And there was a certain nobleman, whose son was sick at Capernaum.

⁴⁷ When he heard that Jesus was come out of Judaea into Galilee, he went unto him, and besought him that he would come down, and heal his son: for he was at the point of death.

⁴⁸ Then said Jesus unto him, Except ye see signs and wonders, ye will not believe.

⁴⁹ The nobleman saith unto him, Sir, come down ere my child die.

⁵⁰ Jesus saith unto him, Go thy way; thy son liveth. And the man believed the word that Jesus had spoken unto him, and he went his way.

⁵¹ And as he was now going down, his servants met him, and told him, saying, Thy son liveth.

⁵² Then enquired he of them the hour when he began to amend. And they said unto him, Yesterday at the seventh hour the fever left him.

⁵³ So the father knew that it was at the same hour, in the which Jesus said unto him, Thy son liveth: and himself believed, and his whole house.

⁵⁴ This is again the second miracle that Jesus did, when he was come out of Judaea into Galilee.

Like the Changing of Water into Wine, this parable of healing also takes place in Galilee. Thus, we're meant to see that its locale intimates an evolution of love solely expressed among blood ties to a broader compass of love-of-strangers. As before, this bears psychological indications that a process of ego is taking place. It's becoming interiorized — it shifts from personal experience to a broader expression of love. Note that the central aspect of this miracle pivots upon the <u>faith</u> of a nobleman: "Jesus therefore said to him, 'Unless you see signs and wonders you will not believe.' The official said to him, 'Sir, come down before my child dies.' Jesus said to him, 'Go; your son will live.' The man believed the word that Jesus spoke to him and went his way."

Faith is certainly not an element typically found in depth psychology. For example, Jung says this about faith: "Faith and knowledge can no more agree than Christians can with one another. Faith is blinding; it is childlike and encourages people to remain children instead of becoming as children. As such, it always involves us in the conflict between faith and knowledge." (C. G. Jung, *Aion*, p. 269.)

Additionally, psychology often concerns developing knowledge of the soul, of what has influenced us, of what lives in our unconscious. For example, Stephan Hoeller, in his book, *The Gnostic Jung and the Seven Sermons to the Dead*, says:

".... the meaning and purpose of life appears to be neither faith, with its emphasis on blind belief and equally blind repression, nor works with their extraverted do-goodism, but rather an interior insight and transformation, in short, a depth-psychological process." (p. 11)

To have faith, of course, means to have trust. The parable of the healing of the nobleman's son exposes a new interior capacity of the ego, the capacity of complete trust. In this case, trust is understood as an act. Faith isn't an intellectual disposition; instead, it's an action, a doing. I *do* trust. And this has the contour of a miracle because the ability to trust isn't typical of ego consciousness. We have to search deeply to find this interior aspect of the ego. Trust doesn't belong to the inherent nature of ego consciousness. Instead, it's a divine element that occurs within the miracle of the healing of the nobleman's son. And, through this act, we understand that we can trust another. I trust you. This is a miracle, the very presence of the power of Christ in ego consciousness. But, it's not automatically present as such. Moreover, it's not present as "content" of ego consciousness; rather, it's potential, It can be there if we orient ourselves towards it. The presence of Christ within the ego makes it possible for us to have conscious trust in others, an act of the transformed ego. In other words, trust is something we do out of ego consciousness — and that, indeed, is a miracle. There's not something within me that makes me feel I can trust you. I step out of myself and trust you. It's something that I must actively do — it doesn't readily present itself.

The Healing of the Sick Man at the Pool of Bethesda (John 5:1-18) — (I am the Door)

After this there was a feast of the Jews; and Jesus went up to Jerusalem.

2 Now there is at Jerusalem by the sheep market a pool, which is called in the Hebrew tongue Bethesda, having five porches.

3 In these lay a great multitude of impotent folk, of blind, halt, withered, waiting for the moving of the water.

4 For an angel went down at a certain season into the pool, and troubled the water: whosoever then first after the troubling of the water stepped in was made whole of whatsoever disease he had.

5 And a certain man was there, which had an infirmity thirty and eight years.

6 When Jesus saw him lie, and knew that he had been now a long time in that case, he saith unto him, Wilt thou be made whole?

7 The impotent man answered him, Sir, I have no man, when the water is troubled, to put me into the pool: but while I am coming, another steppeth down before me.

8 Jesus saith unto him, Rise, take up thy bed, and walk.

9 And immediately the man was made whole, and took up his bed, and walked: and on the same day was the sabbath.

10 The Jews therefore said unto him that was cured, It is the sabbath day: it is not lawful for thee to carry thy bed.

11 He answered them, He that made me whole, the same said unto me, Take up thy bed, and walk.

12 Then asked they him, What man is that which said unto thee, Take up thy bed, and walk?

¹³ And he that was healed wist not who it was: for Jesus had conveyed himself away, a multitude being in that place.

¹⁴ Afterward Jesus findeth him in the temple, and said unto him, Behold, thou art made whole: sin no more, lest a worse thing come unto thee.

¹⁵ The man departed, and told the Jews that it was Jesus, which had made him whole.

¹⁶ And therefore did the Jews persecute Jesus, and sought to slay him, because he had done these things on the sabbath day.

¹⁷ But Jesus answered them, My Father worketh hitherto, and I work.

¹⁸ Therefore the Jews sought the more to kill him, because he not only had broken the sabbath, but said also that God was his Father, making himself equal with God.

When given close attention, it appears that the water in the Bethesda Pool was periodically disturbed either by an underground disturbance or by an influx of new water. This disturbance was attributed to an angel, and the first person to enter the pool after the angel disturbed the water would be healed. Jesus' attention was drawn to one man who had suffered from an illness for thirty-eight years and who spent most of his time waiting by the pool, without ever being able to enter the water first after it was disturbed. Jesus says to this man: "Do you will (thelo, in Greek, means "will") to be well again?"

> 1. Notice that the man is hesitant. He doesn't answer the question.
>
> 2. Notice what Jesus says: "Get up, pick up your

sleeping-mat and walk!"

3. And then, afterward, he says to the man: "See, you are well! Sin no more, that nothing worse befall you.

4. Special mention is made of the fact that this healing occurred on the Sabbath, that the man healed, picked up his mat and walked on the day that was supposed to be for rest. And, further, the Pharisees, hearing the story, said that Christ had violated the Sabbath by working on the day of rest.

The specific Greek word used for sin here is *hamartano*, which means "missing the mark." This man's life was off the mark. We get the sense of that by his hesitation, almost as if he wished to remain ill. Christ has to <u>command</u> him to be healed.

We should note that our ego consciousness is consistently off the mark, taking us in a wrong direction, and trying to make our life the way we think it should be. This is contrary to the way destiny operates; destiny will inevitably lead us into the right experiences that we need to accelerate our deepest level of growth.

Through this miracle, Christ instills a new, interior ego capacity. How do we know when we're "off the mark" in our lives? By this I mean "off the mark" in a spiritual sense. We say that we rely upon our conscience. But, we also know that the ego has strong defenses that will ignore, deny, project onto others, not see, not hear, not listen. What is instilled into ego consciousness through this miracle is a moral capacity. The ego now has a moral capacity to experience when we are going in a spiritual direction that is unhelpful. And note that it comes to us as an inner command. Not a command to *not* do something, but rather as a command *to* do something. The image of the miracle intimates the propensity for us to falter — to not follow the promptings of the soul, just as the man in the miracle doesn't go towards the soul element of water stirred by an angel. We tend to ignore the stirrings of our soul. Also, we tend to avoid any prompting of a more subtle nature, such as following our intuitions, which are often felt as gentle, spiritual promptings.

Importantly and paradoxically, there's an aspect of the ego that confronts us

from within our own egocentricity. Now this is such an uncomfortable situation that it's certainly a miracle! In the story, the man promptly told Jesus' enemies who cured him on the Sabbath. As a result, Jesus was persecuted. This indicates that we don't want to be confronted by our egocentric attitudes. In fact, every time this occurs, we will hear-sense-feel an interior command to move into new terrain on a spiritual level. And, because the miracle occurs on the Sabbath, we're made to understand that when we feel these promptings to move, we should move in ways that are dedicated to God — for, indeed, the Sabbath is the day dedicated to God.

Feeding of the 5,000 (John 6.1-15) — (I am the bread of Life)

After these things Jesus went over the sea of Galilee, which is the sea of Tiberias.

2 And a great multitude followed him, because they saw his miracles which he did on them that were diseased.

3 And Jesus went up into a mountain, and there he sat with his disciples.

4 And the passover, a feast of the Jews, was nigh.

5 When Jesus then lifted up his eyes, and saw a great company come unto him, he saith unto Philip, Whence shall we buy bread, that these may eat?

6 And this he said to prove him: for he himself knew what he would do.

7 Philip answered him, Two hundred pennyworth of bread is not sufficient for them, that every one of them may take a little.

8 One of his disciples, Andrew, Simon Peter's brother, saith unto him,

9 There is a lad here, which hath five barley loaves, and two small fishes: but what are they among so many?

10 And Jesus said, Make the men sit down. Now there was much grass in the place. So the men sat down, in number about five thousand.

11 And Jesus took the loaves; and when he had given thanks, he distributed to the disciples, and the disciples to them that were set down; and likewise of the fishes as much as they would.

12 When they were filled, he said unto his disciples, Gather up the fragments that remain, that nothing be lost.

13 Therefore they gathered them together, and filled twelve baskets with the fragments of the five barley loaves, which remained over and above unto them that had eaten.

14 Then those men, when they had seen the miracle that Jesus did, said, This is of a truth that prophet that should come into the world.

15 When Jesus therefore perceived that they would come and take him by force, to make him a king, he departed again into a mountain himself alone.

This narrative invites us to remember that Christ performs this miracle through the assistance of his twelve disciples. The text says: "And Jesus took the loaves; and when he had given thanks, he distributed them to the disciples, and the disciples to them that were set down; and likewise of the fishes as much as they would." (John 6:11)"

The Church Father, Origin, says of this miracle in his *Commentary on John*: "He was broken up and thinned out" in order to become incarnated into each of us.

Christ as the center of consciousness — as the very structure of ego consciousness — becomes interiorized, and we are filled with a love that confers upon us the ability to extend consciousness. This means that insight, knowledge, intuition, and love can now be endlessly reproduced in the ego. Again, it's important to continually point out that we are all, for the most part, ego-oriented and ego-centered unless a conscious effort is made to experience the presence of Christ as a transformative force. To the extent that we actively seek to be present to this significant, structural alteration of ego, we'll experience the multiplication of spiritual insight and love.

The world becomes experienced as the Body of Christ. In alchemy, this part of the process of alchemical transformation was called *multiplicatio*. When one had achieved the ultimate goal, the making of the philosopher's stone, one of the extraordinary qualities of this stone was that if even the smallest bit of it was projected onto an object, that object turned into gold. In other words, the philosopher's stone was replicated. In terms of ego consciousness, this indicates that projection is necessary. In this case, projection involves experiencing Christ everywhere, within everything, and in everyone. Likewise, in alchemy, the projection of gold is effective because it reveals the invisible gold hidden within all things.

The miracle of the Feeding of the Multitude brings to us an image of the twelve apostles in terms of ego consciousness. In psychology, ego is typically imagined as the center of personality. On the periphery of ego consciousness, depth psychology understands the presence of a shadow, a kind of mid-region between ego consciousness and soul, consisting of all of the aspects of our ego life that are negatively evaluated by us or by others. The shadow doesn't so much reflect soul life, although it's a bridge to soul life. And without inner work, we remain unaware of our shadow because these aspects of ourselves have been excised from consciousness. The miracle of the Feeding of the 5,000, seen from a spiritual-psychological point of view, is a healing of the multiple aspects of our shadow. It's not that we have only twelve such qualities; twelve, in this case, is meant to be an image of the multiplying of ego consciousness. Thus, we not only become aware of our shadow qualities — we see that these multiple aspects of ego are centers of action, centers for offering a spiritual sensibility to the world. In standard depth psychology, coming to terms with the shadow is seen as important, something to be integrated into the ego. The term "integration" carries a quality of the multiple being taken into a singular aspect. However, the miracle of the feeding of the 5,000 shows us something that works in a very different fashion. The one, the spiritual ego, is divided into multiple parts. And, in order for a spiritual sensibility to enter into the world, we're given a new ego capacity that enables our shadow aspect to become the very bread of life!

The Miracle of Christ walking on the water (John 6.16-21) — (I am the seed of the Kingdom of Heaven)

Rudolf Steiner makes an important comment on the translation of this story. He says that the term "walking" is mistranslated: "Modern publishers of the Gospels assign to this chapter the highly superfluous title, "Jesus walks on the sea" — as though that were stated anywhere in this chapter! Where does it say, "Jesus walks on the sea?" It says, "The disciples saw Jesus approaching on the sea."(*The Gospel of St. John and Its Relation to the Other Gospels*, p. 174)

The slight difference outlined by Steiner is quite significant, and makes us reconsider the nature of all of the aforementioned miracles. There is a strong tendency to interpret all of the miracles in a completely materialistic way. We imagine the miracles occurring on the physical level; however, in the view of Rudolf Steiner, they occur on a very different level altogether. Here is what he says concerning this miracle:

"Now, although their physical sight could not reach the Christ, they had the power to see Him, to behold His very form. Christ could become visible at a distance to those whose souls His own had united. His own form is now sufficiently advanced to be seen spiritually. At the moment when the possibility of physical vision disappears, there arises in the disciples all the more intensely the ability to see spiritually — and they see the Christ." (*The Gospel of St. John and its relation to the Other*

Gospels, p. 175).

The capacity to see form, to see the invisible, without translating it back into the physical, is an utterly new capacity of the ego. This miracle conveys the whole sense of the entire Gospel of St. John. Georg Kuhlewind states it in the following way:

"Since the Word now dwells within him, man can see the light — the light which is the radiance of the Logos — without tearing his consciousness from the body and without changing the plane of his consciousness so abruptly to lose his connection with everyday-consciousness, as he had to previously when the human body was left behind by the cognitive principle during the spiritual experience." (*Becoming Aware of the Logos*, p. 41).

The presence of the Word brings to the fore a completely new quality of consciousness, the capacity to be present to the spiritual world without leaving aside the body or leaving aside ego consciousness. We, of course, have to move gradually into this kind of consciousness, and we may not completely do so in this lifetime. However, the presence of this capacity means that humanity has a new task, and that is to work towards the spiritual world by enlarging everyday consciousness. Otherwise, working in outmoded ways will only make it more difficult for individuals and all of humanity to move toward experiencing the Logos.

What is now needed are concentration and image exercises that work out of a fully embodied, conscious soul life that doesn't bypass the ego — but also isn't egotistical. The egotistical sense of the ego must recede while the Logos sense of the ego increases. While these new exercises don't leave the body, we no longer identify the ego with the body. Rather, the ego *is* the Logos, and our work isn't to become conscious of the Logos, but to live within it as fully as possible.

Logos consciousness, this new ego consciousness, makes it known that this miracle is expressed as a consciousness that needs no support, just as Christ approaches the disciples without need for support.

This narrative also discloses the fear of the disciples when they see Christ approaching them. This is a holy fear, a reverential fear. Christ counters their trepidation when he utters, "Do not fear; it is I (ego emi)." Thus, the "I," the Christ-imbued I, instills embodied reverence. Our ordinary consciousness has the potential of being holy consciousness, and our experience of the world and of others has the potential of becoming sacred revelation.

The Healing of the Man Born Blind (John 9) — (I am the Light of the World)

And as Jesus passed by, he saw a man which was blind from his birth.

[2] And his disciples asked him, saying, Master, who did sin, this man, or his parents, that he was born blind?

[3] Jesus answered, Neither hath this man sinned, nor his parents: but that the works of God should be made manifest in him.

[4] I must work the works of him that sent me, while it is day: the night cometh, when no man can work.

[5] As long as I am in the world, I am the light of the world.

[6] When he had thus spoken, he spat on the ground, and made clay of the spittle, and he anointed the eyes of the blind man with the clay,

[7] And said unto him, Go, wash in the pool of Siloam, (which is by interpretation, Sent.) He went his way therefore, and washed, and came seeing.

[8] The neighbours therefore, and they which before had seen him that he was blind, said, Is not this he that sat and begged?

[9] Some said, This is he: others said, He is like him: but he said, I am he.

[10] Therefore said they unto him, How were thine eyes opened?

[11] He answered and said, A man that is called Jesus made clay, and anointed mine eyes, and said unto me, Go to the pool of Siloam, and wash: and I went and washed, and I received sight.

[12] Then said they unto him, Where is he? He said, I know not.

[13] They brought to the Pharisees him that aforetime was blind.

[14] And it was the sabbath day when Jesus made the clay, and opened his eyes.

[15] Then again the Pharisees also asked him how he had received his sight. He said unto them, He put clay upon mine eyes, and I washed, and do see.

[16] Therefore said some of the Pharisees, This man is not of God, because he keepeth not the sabbath day. Others said, How can a man that is a sinner do such miracles? And there was a division among them.

¹⁷ They say unto the blind man again, What sayest thou of him, that he hath opened thine eyes? He said, He is a prophet.

¹⁸ But the Jews did not believe concerning him, that he had been blind, and received his sight, until they called the parents of him that had received his sight.

¹⁹ And they asked them, saying, Is this your son, who ye say was born blind? how then doth he now see?

²⁰ His parents answered them and said, We know that this is our son, and that he was born blind:

²¹ But by what means he now seeth, we know not; or who hath opened his eyes, we know not: he is of age; ask him: he shall speak for himself.

²² These words spake his parents, because they feared the Jews: for the Jews had agreed already, that if any man did confess that he was Christ, he should be put out of the synagogue.

²³ Therefore said his parents, He is of age; ask him.

²⁴ Then again called they the man that was blind, and said unto him, Give God the praise: we know that this man is a sinner.

²⁵ He answered and said, Whether he be a sinner or no, I know not: one thing I know, that, whereas I was blind, now I see.

²⁶ Then said they to him again, What did he to thee? how opened he thine eyes?

²⁷ He answered them, I have told you already, and ye did not hear: wherefore would ye hear it again? will ye also be his disciples?

²⁸ Then they reviled him, and said, Thou art his disciple; but we are Moses' disciples.

²⁹ We know that God spake unto Moses: as for this fellow, we know not from whence he is.

³⁰ The man answered and said unto them, Why herein is a marvellous thing, that ye know not from whence he is, and yet he hath opened mine eyes.

³¹ Now we know that God heareth not sinners: but if any man be a worshipper of God, and doeth his will, him he heareth.

³² Since the world began was it not heard that any man opened the eyes of one that was born blind.

³³ If this man were not of God, he could do nothing.

³⁴ They answered and said unto him, Thou wast altogether born in sins, and dost thou teach us? And they cast him out.

³⁵ Jesus heard that they had cast him out; and when he had found him, he said unto him, Dost thou believe on the Son of God?

³⁶ He answered and said, Who is he, Lord, that I might believe on him?

³⁷ And Jesus said unto him, Thou hast both seen him, and it is he that talketh with thee.

³⁸ And he said, Lord, I believe. And he worshipped him.

³⁹ And Jesus said, For judgment I am come into this world, that they which see not might see; and that they which see might be made blind.

⁴⁰ And some of the Pharisees which were with him heard these words, and said unto him, Are we blind also?

⁴¹ Jesus said unto them, If ye were blind, ye should have no sin: but now ye say, We see; therefore your sin remaineth.

"As long as I am in the world, I am the light of the world." (John 9:5). It is the Logos, Christ, who makes seeing possible; and it is Christ who allows for the conjoining of the seen and the seer. This miracle also extends the meaning of the miracle just considered — that of Christ approaching the apostles on water. There are some rather strange statements made by Christ in the course of this story that can be clarified. For instance, Christ says: "For judgment I came into the world, that those who do not see may see, and that those who see may become blind." (John 9: 39). Valentine Tomberg interprets this passage in the following manner:

"The true and original vision which preceded the Fall was a vertical vision. That is, it was a beholding with the "upper eye" and with the "lower eye" — with the "upper eye" of the reflection of the Logos in the waters above the firmament, and with the "lower eye" of the reflection of the Logos in the waters below the firmament.

However, when through the Fall vision became horizontal, i.e. the 'lower eye' became the sole organ of seeing, then 'Adam and Eve saw that they were naked.' This means that vision became devoid of ideas, i.e. of facts alone…. It became basically cynical. And it was this vision, limited to the bare facts which the man born blind had renounced at the time of his choice of destiny, in order that the true, original vision… might be reinstated in him." (*Covenant of the Heart*, pp. 34-35).

The sense of the passage understood from a spiritual-psychological perspective is that the Logos enters the ego in order to witness the creative act that originates all things; thus, seeing things in a completely literal way will cease. Ironically, it is those who believe they see most clearly (and know everything and possess the truth) who are, in fact, spiritually blind. On the other hand, those who recognize their need and their blindness are the ones who are most open to Christ.

This miracle also reveals something else of importance. The disciples ask Christ whether this man's blindness is due to his sin or the sins of his parents. Christ answers that neither he nor his parents had sinned, but rather that he was born blind so the works of God might be displayed in him. If we hear this in terms of the ego and ego consciousness, it says that the ordinary ego consciousness by which we live is necessary. Thus, there's nothing wrong with ego consciousness; it's not a failing. In fact, ordinary ego consciousness is required in order for there to be a consciousness filled with Light. The spirit of Christ (imaged as Christ's spittle mixed with dirt) joins with the soul of the world (imaged as the blind man washing his eyes in the pool of Siloam). Again, we're called to see that spiritual consciousness is most vividly seen in terms of a transformation of ordinary, ego consciousness rather than a deprecation of it.

This miracle also shows us the importance of realizing that our ordinary ego consciousness is blind. The miracle of seeing fully requires *knowing* that we're blind, and this certainly isn't an easy thing for the ego to admit. To experience this miracle requires that we admit that we are, indeed, blind literalists. The ego can't help but literalize, which means we see things without the nuance borne of seeing the heavenly and the earthly realms together and simultaneously. We must cleanse our own eyes. And then, like the blind man, we, too, will have a story and a history to recall and share.

The Miracle of the Raising of Lazarus from the Dead (John 11) — (I am the Resurrection and the Life)

Now a certain man was sick, named Lazarus, of Bethany, the town of Mary and her sister Martha.

2 (It was that Mary which anointed the Lord with ointment, and wiped his feet with her hair, whose brother Lazarus was sick.)

3 Therefore his sisters sent unto him, saying, Lord, behold, he whom thou lovest is sick.

4 When Jesus heard that, he said, This sickness is not unto death, but for the glory of God, that the Son of God might be glorified thereby.

5 Now Jesus loved Martha, and her sister, and Lazarus.

6 When he had heard therefore that he was sick, he abode two days still in the same place where he was.

7 Then after that saith he to his disciples, Let us go into Judaea again.

8 His disciples say unto him, Master, the Jews of late sought to stone thee; and goest thou thither again?

9 Jesus answered, Are there not twelve hours in the day? If any man walk in the day, he stumbleth not, because he seeth the light of this world.

10 But if a man walk in the night, he stumbleth, because there is no light in him.

11 These things said he: and after that he saith unto them, Our friend Lazarus sleepeth; but I go, that I may awake him out of sleep.

12 Then said his disciples, Lord, if he sleep, he shall do well.

¹³ Howbeit Jesus spake of his death: but they thought that he had spoken of taking of rest in sleep.

¹⁴ Then said Jesus unto them plainly, Lazarus is dead.

¹⁵ And I am glad for your sakes that I was not there, to the intent ye may believe; nevertheless let us go unto him.

¹⁶ Then said Thomas, which is called Didymus, unto his fellow disciples, Let us also go, that we may die with him.

¹⁷ Then when Jesus came, he found that he had lain in the grave four days already.

¹⁸ Now Bethany was nigh unto Jerusalem, about fifteen furlongs off:

¹⁹ And many of the Jews came to Martha and Mary, to comfort them concerning their brother.

²⁰ Then Martha, as soon as she heard that Jesus was coming, went and met him: but Mary sat still in the house.

²¹ Then said Martha unto Jesus, Lord, if thou hadst been here, my brother had not died.

²² But I know, that even now, whatsoever thou wilt ask of God, God will give it thee.

²³ Jesus saith unto her, Thy brother shall rise again.

²⁴ Martha saith unto him, I know that he shall rise again in the resurrection at the last day.

²⁵ Jesus said unto her, I am the resurrection, and the life: he that believeth in me, though he were dead, yet shall he live:

²⁶ And whosoever liveth and believeth in me shall never die. Believest thou this?

²⁷ She saith unto him, Yea, Lord: I believe that thou art the Christ, the Son of God, which should come into the world.

²⁸ And when she had so said, she went her way, and called Mary her sister secretly, saying, The Master is come, and calleth for thee.

²⁹ As soon as she heard that, she arose quickly, and came unto him.

³⁰ Now Jesus was not yet come into the town, but was in that place where Martha met him.

³¹ The Jews then which were with her in the house, and comforted her, when they saw Mary, that she rose up hastily and went out, followed her, saying, She goeth unto the grave to weep there.

³² Then when Mary was come where Jesus was, and saw him, she fell down at his feet, saying unto him, Lord, if thou hadst been here, my brother had not died.

³³ When Jesus therefore saw her weeping, and the Jews also weeping which came with her, he groaned in the spirit, and was troubled.

³⁴ And said, Where have ye laid him? They said unto him, Lord, come and see.

³⁵ Jesus wept.

³⁶ Then said the Jews, Behold how he loved him!

³⁷ And some of them said, Could not this man, which opened the eyes of the blind, have caused that even this man should not have died?

³⁸ Jesus therefore again groaning in himself cometh to the grave. It was a cave, and a stone lay upon it.

³⁹ Jesus said, Take ye away the stone. Martha, the sister of him that was dead, saith unto him, Lord, by this time he stinketh: for he hath been dead four days.

⁴⁰ Jesus saith unto her, Said I not unto thee, that, if thou wouldest believe, thou shouldest see the glory of God?

[41] Then they took away the stone from the place where the dead was laid. And Jesus lifted up his eyes, and said, Father, I thank thee that thou hast heard me.

[42] And I knew that thou hearest me always: but because of the people which stand by I said it, that they may believe that thou hast sent me.

[43] And when he thus had spoken, he cried with a loud voice, Lazarus, come forth.

[44] And he that was dead came forth, bound hand and foot with graveclothes: and his face was bound about with a napkin. Jesus saith unto them, Loose him, and let him go.

[45] Then many of the Jews which came to Mary, and had seen the things which Jesus did, believed on him.

[46] But some of them went their ways to the Pharisees, and told them what things Jesus had done.

[47] Then gathered the chief priests and the Pharisees a council, and said, What do we? for this man doeth many miracles.

[48] If we let him thus alone, all men will believe on him: and the Romans shall come and take away both our place and nation.

[49] And one of them, named Caiaphas, being the high priest that same year, said unto them, Ye know nothing at all,

[50] Nor consider that it is expedient for us, that one man should die for the people, and that the whole nation perish not.

[51] And this spake he not of himself: but being high priest that year, he prophesied that Jesus should die for that nation;

⁵² And not for that nation only, but that also he should gather together in one the children of God that were scattered abroad.

⁵³ Then from that day forth they took counsel together for to put him to death.

⁵⁴ Jesus therefore walked no more openly among the Jews; but went thence unto a country near to the wilderness, into a city called Ephraim, and there continued with his disciples.

⁵⁵ And the Jews' passover was nigh at hand: and many went out of the country up to Jerusalem before the passover, to purify themselves.

⁵⁶ Then sought they for Jesus, and spake among themselves, as they stood in the temple, What think ye, that he will not come to the feast?

⁵⁷ Now both the chief priests and the Pharisees had given a commandment, that, if any man knew where he were, he should shew it, that they might take him.

In approaching the seven miracles of Christ in the Gospel of St. John from a spiritual-psychological perspective, we have been aware that each of these images lives deeply in the soul of every individual. They are all present simultaneously, at the ego level of soul life; however, at the level of soul life, we must make an effort to make them manifest. Such work gradually brings new awareness into everyday ego-consciousness. And, as this begins to happen, it may seem that our usual ways of living in everyday consciousness are breaking down. The enclosed soul begins to dissolve, and this may bring about the discomfort of old memories, old feelings; they will likely rise up both in waking consciousness and in dreams. In short, this is part of the experience of contemplating the Gospel of St. John!

Of the seven miracles, the Raising of Lazarus from the Dead is the miracle that provides the greatest impulse for the manifestation of each of the other miracles within ego consciousness. It also hastens the gradual receding of typical ego consciousness while increasing the ego consciousness filled with Logos.

It is of great importance that the death of Lazarus isn't a typical death. When Lazarus' sister comes to Christ to tell Him of Lazarus's illness, Christ says:

"This illness is not unto death; it is for the glory of God, so that the Son of God may be glorified by means of it." (John 11.4). Lazarus was an individual completely devoted to the glory of God; he devotedly poured forth his entire being. The moment of his unusual death — unusual because he wasn't ill and had no disease and had not aged — was also the moment when the force of Christ filled him completely. (For an exposition of this event, see: Valentin Tomberg, *The New Testament*, pp. 133-139).

When Christ calls into the tomb of Lazarus, this is the call of Life to Earth. But, prior to Christ's arrival at the tomb, Christ, Lazarus' sister, and those surrounding them are all weeping. Christ weeps! And his weeping expresses a fidelity to the Earth. A new life-spirit enters humanity when Christ calls out to Lazarus *"Lazare, deuro exo"* — "Lazarus, come out." It is at this point that it becomes possible for human beings to undergo the transformation of ego life that has been described in various ways through the other miracles in the Gospel of St. John. However, this miracle of the raising of Lazarus from the dead is of central importance. While it takes place last in the sequence of seven miracles, it is the one that lives first in the birth of new ego consciousness.

The way in which this miracle lives within each individual is described above. There is the experience of the old form of ego consciousness dying away, and this dying is concomitant with the emergence of a new kind of ego consciousness, one in which we don't identify ourselves with our body and our body with our ego. Instead, we become vessels filled with the Logos, a consciousness in which a sense and an experience of the presence of the spiritual world fills our everyday consciousness, even as we carry on our daily activities. Tomberg points out that the symbolic sign for this concurrent process of the dying-and-birth is the black cross with seven shining, red roses — the Rose Cross.

In order to work with the 7 miracles in a way that you begin to feel them as inner soul experiences, it's important to increase inner sensitivity. The following meditation is based on discovering that the 7 "I AM" sayings and the seven miracles of the Gospel of St. John correspond to the 7 chakras. This meditation allows you to experience the soul-spirit qualities of the miracles.

This meditation should be done by moving from the crown chakra down. It takes a little while to memorize the" I Am" sayings and the miracles. Until you do so, it is a bit mechanical. But, nonetheless, it's a very important meditation.

1. Focus your consciousness at the crown chakra just above the head. Inwardly say "I am the Resurrection and the Life." Then inwardly say "Christ raises Lazarus from the dead" while picturing that scene.

2. Move your consciousness to the region of the mid-forehead. Inwardly say, "I am the Light of the world." Then inwardly say, "Christ heals the man born blind" while picturing that scene.

3. Move your consciousness to the region of the throat. Inwardly say, "I am the good shepherd." Then inwardly say, "Christ walks on water" while picturing that scene.

4. Move your consciousness to the region of the heart. Inwardly say, "I am the Bread of Life." Then inwardly say, "Christ feeds the five thousand with loaves of bread and fish" while inwardly picturing that scene.

5. Move your consciousness to the region of the solar plexus. Inwardly say, "I am the Door, the Opening and the Exit." Then inwardly say, "Christ heals the cripple at the pool of Bethesda" while inwardly picturing that scene.

6. Move your consciousness to the region of the spleen chakra. Inwardly say, "I am the Way, the Truth, and the Life." Then inwardly say, "Christ heals the Nobleman's son" while inwardly picturing that scene.

7. Move your consciousness to the region of the root chakra. Inwardly say, "I am the True Vine." Then inwardly say, "Christ changes water into wine at the wedding feast of Cana" while inwardly picturing that scene.

Then, remain in silence for as long as you wish, experiencing the presence of these sayings and miracles.

After you have become accustomed to this meditation and can go through it without having to think about the words and pictures and locations, do the meditation each day for week. Then, choose three of the "I Am" sayings and miracles from the Gospel of St. John and write a short description of how each has changed in light of your work in meditation.

Printed in Great Britain
by Amazon

84979010R00036